Aquarius

21 January – 18 February

amber
BOOKS

ASTROLOGICAL SIGN DATES:
The precise start and end times for each sign vary by a day or two from year to year as the Gregorian calendar shifts relative to the tropical year. The dates provided in this book are correct for the year 2020.

If you are unsure of the Zodiac sign for your specific birth year, visit: www.yourzodiacsign.com.

Aquarius

21 January – 18 February

A guide to understanding yourself, your friendships and finding your true love

This edition first published in 2020 by
Amber Books Ltd
United House
North Road
London N7 9DP
United Kingdom
www.amberbooks.co.uk
Instagram: amberbooksltd
Facebook: amberbooks
Twitter: @amberbooks

ISBN: 978-1-83886-031-8

Project Editor: Sarah Uttridge
Design: Zoë Mellors

Picture Credits:
All illustrations by Fabbri Publications except the following:
Dreamstime: 37 (Retrocoloring)
Shutterstock: 30 (CataVic), 32 (La Puma), 35 (Slonomysh), 41 (Angel Soler Gollonet)

Printed and bound in China

TRADITIONAL CHINESE BOOKBINDING

This book has been produced using traditional Chinese bookbinding techniques, using a method that was developed during the Ming Dynasty (1368–1644) and remained in use until the adoption of Western binding techniques in the early 1900s. In traditional Chinese binding, single sheets of paper are printed on one side only, and each sheet is folded in half, with the printed pages on the outside. The book block is then sandwiched between two boards and sewn together through punched holes close to the cut edges of the folded sheets.

Contents

Introduction

Aquarius

21 January–18 February

Sign: The Water Carrier

Ruling Planet: Uranus and Saturn

Gender: Masculine

Element: Air

Quality: Fixed

Compatibility: Pisces and Capricorn

Non-compatibility: Almost no one – at least in theory

Every man, woman and child is born with a distinct and different destiny. There are no exceptions. Everyone has cosmic significance and a part to play in the life of the universe This is innate and inescapable, and goes beyond the tiny boundaries of nation, creed and colour.

As we live out our lives on planet Earth we are, however unknowingly, acting in a greater drama and reacting to impulses that come from distant astronomical bodies, stars and planets millions of light years away. Sceptics pour scorn on the idea that far-distant Saturn, for example, can have any effect on our lives, as the ancient art and science of astrology teaches. But the fact is that we are sparks of energy inhabiting bodies made of the same stuff as the stars, responding like tiny radios to the distant messages they send to Earth.

Each infant carries within it a double blueprint for life: its genetic programming and the pattern of character that comes from the astrological 'clock' that was set in motion at the moment of birth. No one knows the full extent of genetic influence, although it seems to be astonishingly far-reaching, but the power of the horoscope has been well known to the wisest men and women for many centuries.

Our Sun and Moon signs provide essential inside information about our destinies. They reveal the secrets of who we really are, and why we are here, laying out before us our potential, the sort of joys and achievements our characteristics may bring about, and warn us of problems to be overcome through the triumph of free will.

Read this book with an open mind and discover who you really are.

The Elements

Up to the beginning of the Age of Enlightenment – the modern scientific era – in the 18th century, it was commonly believed that everything, including human beings, was made up of the four elements: Earth, Air, Fire and Water. These were thought of as the building blocks of life, and each astrological sign had a predominance of one or another. Each created its common characteristics, although too much of any of the elements can produce an unbalanced personality.

Air Signs

The Air signs are Gemini, Libra and Aquarius. These inspirational, communicative signs of the zodiac can talk a lot of 'hot air', and their ability to cause a 'wind of change' to run through society is a mixed blessing.

This tendency is viewed with horror by the Earth signs, to whom all chance is fraught with danger. Often the Air signs are blown this way and that by sudden enthusiasms and conflicting, contradictory opinions, but they can throw new light on apparently intractable problems. It is their influence that helps sweep away outmoded ways of doing things, bringing in all manner of brave new worlds. Geminians talk and act fast, and live life at a furious pace, often doing several things at once – one of which is forever talking on the telephone. Librans are more cool and collected, the arbiters and diplomats of the zodiac, but they can be great ditherers, prone to sudden reversals of opinion.

Aquarians, the idealists and New Agers of the zodiac, can move swiftly if their crusading zeal is fully engaged, and their motivation is razor-sharp. If they feel something is best for humankind, they will go for it, dropping everything else, including all thoughts of personal comfort or gain. However, they can also be irritatingly nebulous and 'airy-fairy', often lost in their dreams of creating a brave new world while failing to make their mark on this one.

Air Signs

Gemini

Libra

Aquarius

Colours of the Zodiac

Traditionally, each sign of the zodiac has its own colour, which is believed to be 'lucky' or magically empowered for those born under that particular sign. In general, the colours are associated with the ruling planets and are symbolic of their attributes. Many people find that they feel most comfortable when wearing their sign's colours, and often choose them without knowing their full astrological background.

Aquarius

Ruling Planet: Uranus.

Colour: This is unique in the zodiac for traditionally having all the colours of the rainbow – sometimes all at the same time.

The Angelic Hierarchy

According to ancient tradition, each planet is governed by one of the great archangels, who are also rulers of certain aspects of human life. The box below lists the planet that they rule, the areas over which they have influence and their special day of the week.

Uriel

Archangel of Uranus.

Governs: Aquarius.

Rules: Magic, astrology, mysticism and sudden change.

Day: Uriel is not associated with any particular day.

The Genders

Traditionally, the twelve signs of the zodiac are divided into Masculine and Feminine, although of course both men and women are born into each.

The characteristics were assigned to the genders aeons ago, well before modern feminism or political correctness, and may now seem old-fashioned to many. However, the signs do seem to be grouped according to the appropriate gender.

The Masculine Signs

The Masculine signs are Aries, Gemini, Leo, Libra, Sagittarius and Aquarius. Masculine traits do tend to be accentuated in the Fire signs, which are Aries, Leo and Sagittarius.

Masculine signs are dominant and assertive, often to the point of being pugnacious and extroverted. They are natural leaders and rulers, showing fiery initiative, and are fiercely protective of others in their care. They are pioneers and visionaries, conquerors of new lands and the first to achieve great things. They tend to tackle things themselves and can be impatient with others who are less assertive.

Negatively, Masculine signs can be egotistical, arrogant and cruel, and dismissive of the needs and feelings of others. They can often prove to be trouble-makers and rebels – violent, belligerent and inclined to subversion.

The Ruling Planets

Until the 18th century, astrologers knew only the planets of our solar system that could be seen with the naked eye: Mercury, Venus, Mars, Jupiter and Saturn. (For the purposes of astrology, the Sun and the Moon are also counted as planets even though the Sun is a star and the Moon is the satellite of Earth.) Uranus was discovered in 1781, Neptune in 1846 and Pluto was first seen in 1930. Many astrologers believe that the existence of other heavenly bodies – such as the rumoured Vulcan, which hypothetically exists within the orbit of Mercury – is about to be confirmed. Astrologers will then have to agree which signs these 'new' planets will rule, and what human characteristics their discovery will accentuate.

Uranus

In Greek mythology, Uranus was the son of the Great Mother, from whose incestuous mating were born all the creatures of the Earth.

Uranus governs Aquarius, bestowing the ability to be forward-looking, original and idealistic. The negative aspects of Uranus as a ruling planet are its tendency to make Aquarians too eager to sweep away the old, to be shocking and to seek 'kicks' in unusual and even dangerous ways.

About Uranus

Four times the size of Earth, Uranus was discovered in 1781 by William Herschel. It is nearly 2875 million km (1785 million miles) from the Sun, which it orbits every 84 years. Uranus is surrounded by many rings and has four moons.

Uranus has no sacred day.

About Saturn

At 120,000 km (74,600 miles) in diameter, Saturn is the second-largest planet in our solar system. It is 1427 million km (887 million miles) away from the Sun, which it takes 29 years to orbit.

The day sacred to Saturn is, of course, Saturday.

Saturn

The god Saturn originally governed the agricultural arts and skills, but later gave his name to one of Rome's festivals – Saturnalia, in which winter was enlivened with music, dancing and feasting.

Saturn rules Capricorn (and, more controversially, Aquarius), bestowing the mixed blessing of great karmic lessons on those born under the sign of the Goat. It can make its subjects inclined to be narrow in outlook, but it can also bring tenacity and wisdom.

The Qualities

In addition to the influence of gender, the elements and the planets, each sign of the zodiac is affected by having an intrinsic quality – Cardinal, Fixed or Mutable.

Fixed Quality

Individuals born under a Fixed sign have an inherent disposition towards tradition, convention and stability. They hate change and often refuse to adapt to new circumstances. These people are not happy taking the initiative or being in situations that require a quick-fire response. Fixed signs also tend to have conventional, conservative opinions and find it hard to move with the times. However, they do tend to be reliable and down to earth.

Aquarius

At first sight, this progressive, idealistic sign would seem to be the antithesis of Fixed. However, many Aquarians are remarkably set in their ways, even though those ways may seem unorthodox. For example, there are still many Aquarian hippies living in communes. They are the backbone of what might be called the New Orthodoxy, espousing anything that fits their idealism, and rejecting everything that does not.

Signs and Symbols

Most people are familiar with the zodiac 'zoo' – the collection of symbols that represent the twelve signs. These images reflect the characteristics traditionally assigned to each sign and contain a wealth of knowledge about its true nature.

Each sign of the zodiac is represented by a symbol – the twin fish for Pisces, for example. No one is sure exactly when or why the symbols were chosen, although some authorities believe they date from Sumeria or Mesopotamia, 4000 years before Jesus Christ. The priest-astrologers of the ancient world were the first to impose recognizable patterns on the great constellations – Leo the Lion being one example.

Today, seeing such shapes in the stars may seem fanciful, but thousands of years ago imaginations were more poetic, and many myths told of magical animals, such as the dragon, which had strange powers to influence everyday human life.

Although the ancient Egyptians left few astrological records, they were almost unique in antiquity for worshipping archetypal, animal-headed gods. However, these strange hybrid gods – half-human, half-animal – were worshipped as aspects of one God. Contrary to the general belief that the Egyptians were idolaters, their religion was basically monotheistic. Each statue represented an aspect of the one true God.

Since they were established, the signs have remained unchanged, although there was a movement in the Middle Ages to change the sign of Aquarius to the sign of John the Baptist – presumably because of the connection with water.

The twelve signs of the zodiac do seem particularly apt on the whole, and accurately reflect the archetypal character of Sun sign types. The great Swiss psychoanalyst Carl Gustav Jung (1875–1961) believed that, deep in our psyches, humanity shares a collective unconscious – a set of archetypal images, which, at a profound level, we all understand. The signs of the zodiac form part of this pool of images, conveying eternal truths to our unconscious minds.

Signs and Symbols

Aries

Taurus

Gemini

Cancer

Leo

Virgo

Libra

Scorpio

Sagittarius

Capricorn

Aquarius

Pisces

Aquarius The Water Carrier

Usually depicted as a young man pouring water from his vessel, Aquarius evokes feelings of compassion, refreshment and rest after a hard struggle. There is also the resonance of a constant flow of ideas or good fortune.

Travellers crossing arid wastes might feel their hearts lift up at the sight of the water carrier; they are refreshed and perhaps inspired by him, reinvigorated before resuming their journey. It is a potent symbol for the idealistic and humanitarian Aquarian.

In ancient times, the Egyptian goddess Isis was the water carrier: she was often depicted as holding two jars, constantly pouring a stream of life-giving water from one to the other. This image became incorporated into the symbolism of Temperance in the Major Arcana of the Tarot cards (and, in some packs, in the Star).

For thousands of years before the building of the Aswan Dam in 1960–4, Egypt was totally dependent on the River Nile for its livelihood. Water was deemed to be very precious, which is why only royalty and certain priesthoods had their own pools, and why water was the central element in their sacred ritual of baptism. They had practised the rite of confession of sins and the symbolic cleansing by immersion many centuries before John the Baptist (who had his headquarters in Alexandria in upper Egypt) took it into Judaea.

In the Middle Ages, there were moves to rename this sign 'John the Baptist' but they failed – perhaps because it would have been too confusing, or because his feast day, on 24 June, does not fall within the span of Aquarius.

Astrologers are uncertain about exactly when the Age of Aquarius will transpire. Some believe it has already dawned, while others believe it will not begin for another two or three hundred years. However, whenever a new Great Year arrives, its influence is always felt many years beforehand. Either way, therefore, we have already begun to feel the effects of the Age of Aquarius.

The Sun in Aquarius

Sun sign Aquarians are friendly, idealistic, independent and humanitarian. That said, they are also the most varied set of individuals within one zodiacal group, so it is difficult to make generalizations about them. However, what is certain is that they tend to be extremely capable, kind and charitable and very forward-looking. After all, the next Great Year is the Age of Aquarius, when these people will come into their own.

Aquarians are natural New Agers, born astrologers and vegetarian eco-warriors, always eager to improve themselves and the world around them, and well aware of the spiritual side to life. They frequently hold strong political views, and often mount campaigns against some form of injustice, or join groups such as Greenpeace or Amnesty International. Usually pacifist, Sun sign Aquarians can be relied upon to be leaders of the alternative scene and courageous challengers of Establishment values. Many of them also hold strong, but sometimes off-beat, religious or spiritual views, and are fond of philosophical debate.

The brave, free-spirited Aquarians are always true friends to the downtrodden, but find it hard to translate all that 'love and light' into close personal relationships. Aquarians may be 'tree huggers', but they are often appallingly bad at creating a loving environment for themselves. For them, charity rarely begins at home.

Although they are good original thinkers and idiosyncratic in many ways, Sun sign Aquarians can seem eccentric. They will, however, be mostly

Personality traits of Aquarians

Positive	*Negative*
Friendly	Stubborn
Independent	Unpredictable
Humanitarian	Impatient
Kind	Inconsistent
Charitable	Don't conform to rules
Supportive	Contrary
Creative	

oblivious to the sly nudgings and criticism of others. Once they have found a lifestyle and, more importantly, a cause, to fight for, they will stick to it obdurately. They can be contrary, though, and expect others to understand their sudden changes of direction, before they settle down again on their chosen life path.

Aquarius is an Air sign, and those born under this sign need their personal space, both literally and figuratively. They hate limits and react very badly to being told what to do, although they can often be surprisingly dictatorial themselves.

Appearance

Sun sign Aquarians come in many different shapes and sizes, but they tend to share attractive, clean-cut looks and a proud bearing. They have open, attentive and sympathetic expressions, and a ready smile which shows off their excellent teeth to advantage. Those born under the sign of the Water Carrier tend to be slim, fairly muscular and bronzed in summer. Even those who take no exercise and eat junk food seem to be naturally at ease with their bodies and, fortunately, rarely get fat.

Many Aquarians wear unusual outfits such as hippy gear or floating New Age kaftans and most would claim to be completely uninterested in something as materialistic and unspiritual as fashion. However, even those who wear thrift shop rejects somehow manage to look noble and set apart from the crowd.

Health

Aquarians' lungs are particularly sensitive to cigarette smoke and air pollution, so they should be careful to avoid these wherever possible. Similarly, they can suffer from allergies

more than most, and should have them checked out by a reputable naturopath.

Traditionally vulnerable to problems with their legs and ankles, Sun sign Aquarians should take care to wear proper protective footwear when hiking, climbing or exploring caves. Another problem area is their circulation, which they should nurture with brisk exercise (especially in winter), massage, warm baths and daily supplements of ginkgo, cod liver oil and evening primrose oil.

Career

Aquarians can turn their hands very successfully to most things, since they are very determined individuals. They can turn their chosen cause into a career while remaining technically unemployed. In a perverse kind of way, some see living off benefits as noble, direct action against a repressive capitalist system. Of course, this sort of Aquarian is relatively rare, but they tend to be so picturesque and newsworthy that they frequently get noticed.

Most are hard-working, perhaps even driven, in their chosen field. Many choose rather unusual or esoteric careers – astrology being one of them – and can often be found at New Age festivals, extolling the virtues of a new gadget that they have invented that will ease all aches and pains. They are best at work that involves them in improving the lot of humanity in some way, and make excellent counsellors and advisers, social workers or charity administrators.

Traditionally, Aquarians are non-materialistic people, but this is not necessarily so. They can be proud individuals who enjoy social and professional status and its perks, such as large cars, comfortable houses and expensive holidays. They enjoy the freedom that comes with money and can be wretched when it runs out. However, they are not grasping or given to signing up for pension plans and insurance policies when young, like Capricornians or Virgoans. They see life as a series of golden opportunities to make the world a happier place – if money happens to come their way, so much the better.

The best careers for Aquarians

- Social worker
- Charity administrator
- Teacher
- Software developer
- Computer programmer
- Research scientist
- Environmental engineer

Aquarians are independent and logical. Their real talents frequently belie their rather unworldly image. Aquarians value education and often do well at university or college, and they travel widely to improve their knowledge of the way others live. With this experience behind them, they are natural problem-solvers, with a strong practical streak and a marked ability to think laterally. They are forever coming up with astonishingly simple, yet elegant, solutions to apparently intractable problems that have stumped others for days, and are not afraid to roll up their sleeves to show them how it can be done.

Aquarians make good teachers and are constantly concerned about how their pupils will turn out, helping them along as best they can. They have a real sense of building the future in the here and now, and realize that the best way of building a fair and decent society is by educating the adults of tomorrow.

Despite their rather airy-fairy image, Aquarians are surprisingly adept with technology, realizing that it is the way forward. This is the key to their thinking. They rarely look back and instead believe that the future is all-important. For them, today's exciting developments will be tomorrow's reality. For this reason, Aquarians can often be found working in futuristic careers, such as information technology and satellite and space probes or conducting research into dolphin communication.

Aquarians have a great need to push back the frontiers of human knowledge. They see progress as the great challenge but recognize that there is a price to pay, such as the terrible human and environmental results of the Industrial Revolution. Their brave new world will be caring, compassionate and informed, and they are willing to work hard to ensure that it comes about.

Relationships

Aquarians tend not to be very good at close relationships, despite all their caring-and-sharing attitudes. They tend to be wary of emotion, often misconstruing it as sentiment that makes irritating demands on their affections. In their minds, they belong to the world, not to one partner or family.

Aquarians need tolerance for their peculiarities, and a large measure of independence, so much so that many of them choose to remain unattached, even though they enjoy having a large variety of passionate relationships. In many respects, they are happier with friends and co-crusaders than with life partners, but if they do enter that elusive lasting relationship they can finally blossom and turn out to be very loyal.

Often, Aquarians are simply too busy rushing from one campaign to the next to stop and notice the love-light in someone else's eyes. All too often, they mistake a desire for personal closeness as a willingness to carry the banners. However, no one should underestimate Sun sign Aquarians. They are by no means obtuse, just rushed off their feet. Once they realize that they are being pursued romantically, they may be amused or irritated, but are rarely won over immediately.

There is something decidedly superior about Aquarians, no matter how friendly and egalitarian they seem to be, or think they are. They have a detached, slightly quizzical air, and often assume that they are giving humanity the benefit of their expertise. This can make them seem attractively mysterious to some, but it can also be very off-putting for others who do not necessarily appreciate being spoken to from on high.

Aquarians can make eccentric parents, expressing themselves in slightly oddball activities. Sometimes there is an element of role reversal: they are the headstrong 'child', while their children are the ones who are comparatively prim and proper. Aquarians are always encouraging their offspring to be bold and experimental and to espouse humanitarian and ecological causes almost before they can walk. Sometimes Aquarian parents are so keen to free their children from the yoke of convention that they take them travelling the world or simply expose them to an unusual home life – in a commune, for example.

Aquarian homes may be neat and bright, and superficially appear much like many other houses in their neighbourhood, but there will usually be something different about them. It may just be their large collection of crystals sparkling in every room, the patch of deliberately untended garden that is home to a variety of wildlife, or the solar panels on the roof. However, it is usually the Aquarian lifestyle that differentiates their homes from those of their neighbours. Colourful people are forever coming and going. Their garden will almost certainly be the scene of some interesting activities – Wiccan celebrations of the New Moon perhaps, or the building of a sauna.

Ideal Partner

Anyone who is also an idealistic free spirit will be suitable for an Aquarian. They detest emotional blackmail, so clingers such as the more badly aspected Cancerian need not apply. Sometimes they respond well to Pisceans, especially if they have a strong Aquarian aspect in their charts, and the same applies to well-grounded Capricornians. In general, though, Aquarians are so individualistic that they could – at least in theory – settle down with almost anyone. However, although the Water Carrier themselves may well be happy with a long-term commitment, the same may not be true of the other half of the relationship.

Compatibility in Relationships

Aries

20 March–19 April

These two signs share world-saving ambitions and can have powerful sexual magnetism, but it may not last long.

Capricorn

21 December–20 January

Oddly staid and cautious Capricornians can succeed in winning the love and protection of Aquarians.

Cancer

21 June–21 July

Cancerians can provide emotional support as long as they are not too clingy or excessively emotional.

Taurus

20 April–20 May

Taureans are disconcerted by Aquarian conventionality and rebellion, and will usually steer clear of it.

Libra

23 September–22 October

Librans may fall under the Aquarian spell, but it may be hero-worship rather than love that fuels the relationship.

Leo

22 July–22 August

Leonine nobility may be appealing, but their grandness cuts no ice with egalitarian Aquarians.

Scorpio
23 October–21 November

Scorpians' interest in deep, mystical subjects appeals to New Age Aquarians, but can be too dark for peace-lovers.

Virgo
23 August–22 September

Aquarians may mock safe, steady Virgoans' obsession with analysis and order as being too retentive.

Aquarius
21 January–18 February

Two world-changing humanitarians might get on, unless their egos are too demanding for such a union.

Sagittarius
22 November–20 December

These two signs are similarly rebellious and free-spirited, but Sagittarian indiscipline may threaten the grand plan.

Gemini
21 May–20 June

Aquarians understand the Geminian restlessness and drive, but add their own, more profound idealism.

Pisces
19 February–19 March

Dreamy, otherworldly Pisceans can find lasting love with mystical Aquarians, who will overlook their intensity.

The Aquarian Child

Children born under the sign of the Water Carrier are friendly and open and need to be free and independent from an early age. Sometimes, they can be too friendly, and need to be educated about the dangers of talking to strangers as soon as they are able to understand.

No Sun sign Aquarian will be totally happy in a highly regimented or over-disciplined school environment. 'Progressive' schools – run, for instance, under the Montessori system – were made for Aquarians. They need to express their creativity and love of nature, and to become involved in local charities when quite young. Aquarians are superb at inventing new and effective ways of fundraising, and should be encouraged to take the lead in this at school and in the local community. Their initiative, energy and unfailing good humour are often an inspiration to others. It is also essential, early practice for all the committee work and philanthropy that they will be involved with in later life.

However, Aquarian children can be worriers, brooding not only about their own problems, whether real or imagined, but also about the state of the world. Troubling news reports can upset them for days, and the parents of Aquarians should take this into account, and treat them accordingly.

Aquarian children have a great need to be taken seriously and should never be mocked or teased. They genuinely appreciate heart-to-heart talks with their parents and positively thrive on family discussions, which give them the opportunity to thrash out problems and plan the way forward. They must feel, however, that their contributions are genuinely valued.

Famous Aquarians

Charles Dickens

Franz Schubert

Paul Newman

Emile Zola

Christian Dior

John McEnroe

Sonny Bono

Humphrey Bogart

Eva Braun

Robert Burns

Lord Byron

Anton Chekhov

Charles Darwin

James Dean

Frederick Delius

Abraham Lincoln

Wolfgang Amadeus Mozart

Ronald Reagan

Franklin D. Roosevelt

George 'Babe' Ruth

Finding Your Sun Sign (2020 dates)

Aries	20 March–19 April*
Taurus	20 April–20 May
Gemini	21 May–20 June
Cancer	21 June–21 July
Leo	22 July–22 August
Virgo	23 August–22 September
Libra	23 September–22 October
Scorpio	23 October–21 November
Sagittarius	22 November–20 December
Capricorn	21 December–20 January
Aquarius	21 January–18 February
Pisces	19 February–19 March

*The dates provided in this book reflect the year 2020.
Dates may vary by a day or two from year to year.